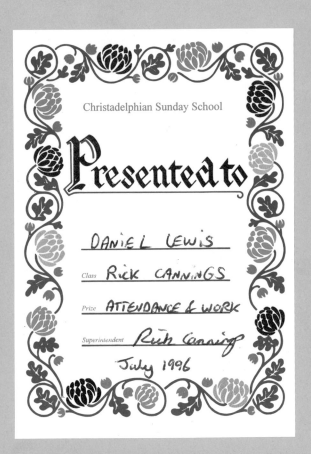

Christadelphian Sunday School

Presented to

DANIEL LEWIS

Class RICK CANNINGS

Prize ATTENDANCE & WORK

Superintendent Rick Cannings

July 1996

AMAZING DISCOVERIES
in Bible Lands

PHOTOGRAPHS
by David Currie

ALSO
J. MAHON 2
SP 4, 5, 39 44 (top), 46 (right)
J. BAILDAM 41 (top)
M. WALKER 44 (bottom),
46 (left), 74 (top)
A. R. RODD 47 (top), 56
D. N. MARSHALL 43, 45,
64, 71, 77

All scripture quotations are
from the New International
Version published by
Hodder and Stoughton,
unless otherwise stated.
Those marked NKJV are
from the New King James
Version published by
Thomas Nelson, Inc.

Copyright ©1995 David Currie
First published 1995

ISBN 1-873796-52-8

Published by
Autumn House Limited
Alma Park, Grantham
Lincs., NG31 9SL
England

AMAZING DISCOVERIES
in Bible Lands

FOR OVER A century the science of Archaeology has interested, intrigued and instructed millions of people. Nations throughout the world have discovered much about their past through the spade of the archaeologist. However, there has been a special interest in the significant biblical archaeological finds of the Middle East — often called the Bible Lands. The present-day nations of Egypt, Iran, Iraq, Israel, Lebanon, Jordan and Syria were much travelled by the heroes and nations of the Old Testament. Cyprus, Greece, Italy and Turkey are added in the arena of the New Testament Scriptures as the early Christian Church emerged and expanded to significance. In these countries dauntless archaeologists have made remarkable discoveries which have commanded world-wide interest and given a greater understanding to the Bible's background.

This presentation in pictures, commentary and scriptural text is an endeavour to direct the reader to the awe-inspiring wonders of some biblical teachings and predictions which have been favourably supported by the archaeologist's spade.

As you travel with me by camera and narrative, I trust that you will not only enjoy the experience but also be encouraged and inspired by the message contained in these pages.

A. DAVID C. CURRIE

DEDICATED to my wife Gaya who has travelled with me and shared in the joys of a greater knowledge of how people lived and how the Scriptures have brought meaning to so many lives.

THANKS to Dr. Bjornar J. Storfjell who has given a major portion of his life to biblical archaeology and assisted in checking the manuscript of this book. However, if there remain any obscurities they belong to me!

AMAZING DISCOVERIES
in Bible Lands

CONTENTS

Iraq

THIS ANCIENT COUNTRY has been a 'gold mine' for biblical archaeologists. It was the centre for the ancient kingdom of Babylon that came to prominence in the seventh to sixth centuries BC under the leadership of King Nebuchadnezzar II. Let's travel through some of its ancient riches!

UR OF THE CHALDEES AND ABRAHAM

To get to Ur was never easy! Either a train that filled with dust each time it moved out of a station, or a minibus that had to be driven through dust storms. It has been almost impossible to get there since the Gulf War. However, for somebody interested in both the Bible and archaeology it was a must and we made it twice! The place is only mentioned four times in Scripture but it was the city where Abraham was born. He is recognized as the physical and spiritual father of the Jews and Muslims, and the spiritual father of Christians.

Genesis 11:31: 'Terah took his son Abram, his grandson Lot son of Haran, and his daughter-in-law Sarai, the wife of his son and together they set out from Ur of the Chaldeans to go to Canaan.'

1 The Temple tower (Ziggurat) located in Abraham's city of Ur.   2 The citizens of Ur worshipped animals — in this case the golden calf.   3 A beautiful mosaic of lapis lazuli (opaque, azure to deep blue gemstones of lazurite) with red limestone and shell, found in one of the royal graves.   4 The golden head-dress worn by a lady in waiting of Queen Shubaid of Ur.   5 When Abraham left Ur, he and his family exchanged their 'modern' homes to live in tents that would have looked like this bedouin tent.

The home city of Abraham was excavated by Sir Leonard Woolley. Prior to this discovery many writers had pictured Abraham and his times as quite primitive. However, this discovery conclusively shows that Abraham was not born in a city of tents but came from a city that boasted a sewage system, a library, law courts and schools. Situated on the Euphrates river it was complete with harbour installations, and these helped to make it a significant trading city. You may see in the Baghdad Archaeological Museum and the British Museum tablets and artifacts from Ur of about four thousand years ago. Sir Leonard Woolley certainly discovered a city having progressive ideas and advanced programmes.

ASSYRIA'S NINEVEH

We travel to the north of Iraq to find Nineveh. Its great walls, across the Tigris river from the modern city of Mosul, have been uncovered and in some places rebuilt. They are seven and a half miles

7

long. Is there any wonder that Jonah the prophet describes this city as 'exceedingly great'? Again the archaeologist's spade has confirmed this assertion. Massive gates welcomed friends or kept out foes. Nineveh was the heart and pride of the Assyrian empire, at the height of its power from the ninth to the seventh centuries BC and ruled over by powerful kings such as Esarhaddon (2 Kings 19:32, etc.), Tiglath-Pileser (2 Kings 15:29, etc.) and Ashurbanipal (Ezra 4:10).

Ashurbanipal was a great book lover and over 20,000 tablets have been found in his famous library. Most of these are in the British Museum. From these tablets we have learned more about the ancient world than from any other source discovered in Bible lands.

SARGON II

While the Scriptures — Isaiah 20:1 — mention Sargon, the king of Assyria, historians could not place him at all. Some even criticized the Scriptures for mentioning an unknown name. However, while the Bible was not written as a history text book, its precision over Sargon II is now acclaimed.

8

3

4

miles north and discovered the palace and city of Sargon II which, all told, covered around 295 hectares (730 acres).

Sargon's son, Sennacherib, ruled for twenty-five years from 705 BC. He was best known in secular history for his infamous battle against Babylon, 689 BC. However, he spent a long time taking the city of Lachish (2 Kings 18:13, 14, 17). This victory is well recorded on the alabaster reliefs found in the British Museum.

NEBUCHADNEZZAR'S BABYLON

Babylonia was a very ancient kingdom, but it was under Nebuchadnezzar II that it reached its zenith, around 600 BC. The Euphrates river flowed through his capital, the walled city of Babylon. This old ruin is about fifty miles south of

Sargon's palace, texts using his name and a relief of his person were first discovered by Emile Botta, the French consul to Mosul. He started digging at Nineveh but became discouraged because he could not find anything of value. He moved ten

1 One of the impressive gates of old Nineveh.

2 Modern-day children tend their sheep where the walls of Nineveh once stood.

3 Assyrian soldiers from Nineveh beautifully depicted in bas-relief brickwork.

4 A bas-relief winged bull with a king's head from the palace of Sargon II.

5 The excavated remains of Nebuchadnezzar II's palace at Babylon.

5

Baghdad, the capital of Iraq. Nebuchadnezzar was responsible for the captivity of the Kingdom of Judah in Palestine and took many of its inhabitants to Babylon as captives. Daniel was one prisoner who eventually rose to prominence in both the Babylonian Empire and the Persian Empire that followed (Daniel 1 and Daniel 6:1, 2).

We travelled south of Babylon over the plain of Shinar. At the southern end of the plain we were quite amazed when we saw the famous ziggurat rebuilt by Nebuchadnezzar II. We could see his name on most of the bricks that we picked up. Today it is called Birs Nimrud though in ancient times it was known as Borsippa. The word Birs is a shortened version of Borsippa. There is no evidence, as some have thought, that the Tower of Babel was built in Borsippa. It was most likely in the part of old Babylon identified by Herodotus, the Greek historian.

The temple-tower built by King Nebuchadnezzar II is about 27 kms

1 The reconstruction of Babylon's Ishtar Gate.
2 Sunset over the River Euphrates as it flows past Babylon.
3 The lion over man — symbol of the greatness of Babylon — found in a swamp in the old city.

1

(17 miles) from his golden city of Babylon. It was once very much higher than it is today. Weather-related erosion, including fierce lightning, has taken off the top of the tower and fused many of its bricks together with red-hot heat.

DURA AND BIRS NIMRUD
(DANIEL AND HIS FRIENDS)

Between the city of Babylon and Birs Nimrud is the large plain of Dura. Here King Nebuchadnezzar assembled nobles and representatives from the provinces and commanded them to worship his new golden image. Shadrach, Meshach and Abed-Nego, Daniel's friends, covenanted to be faithful to the God of heaven. In so doing, however, they received the wrath of the king for not obeying his decree that commanded his subjects to bow down to the huge golden image.

The three Hebrews were thrown into a fiery furnace heated seven times hotter than usual for this occasion. The king

3

noticed that they were untouched by the fire and that there was a fourth person in the furnace with them. He then exclaimed that the fourth person was like the Son of man. It is amazing how God revealed to the king His authority over all elements and His loving care for His faithful servants (Daniel 3).

1 All that remains — the heaps of Babylon — as predicted in Scripture. **2** Samarra is 70 kms (43 miles) north of Baghdad. Its 1,000-year-old temple tower is used by artists as a model for drawings of the tower of Babel. **3** The now famous Gilgamesh epic from Babylon — it contains some similarities to the flood story of Genesis 6.

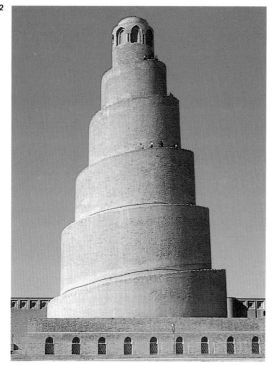

Is there evidence of a fiery furnace at Babylon? While a number of stories have circulated concerning the discovery of a furnace, these have not yet been corroborated.

However, there is at least one cuneiform text that reveals that Babylon used one form of capital punishment by throwing criminals into a fiery furnace. This also lines up with Jeremiah 29:21, 22 (NKJV) where Jeremiah predicts that the false prophets, Zedekiah and Ahab, would be 'roasted in the fire' by Nebuchadnezzar.

SAMARRA AND ITS ZIGGURAT

North of Baghdad is the town of Samarra. This town contains the most colourful tiled mosques in Iraq. Most visitors come to see a relatively modern ziggurat, built about a thousand years ago. The spiral minaret at Samarra is often used as an artist's model for the tower of Babel. There are no known towers from the biblical period or even earlier, which resemble this spiral minaret. Most that have been found are square at the base but did not end up in a point like the pyramids of Egypt. They were generally known as temple towers, such as the one at Ur of the Chaldees.

Egypt

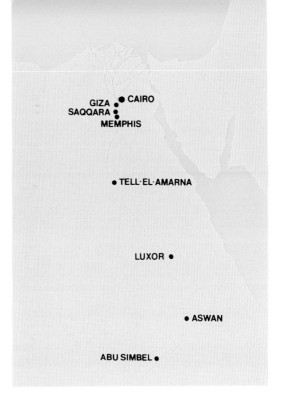

EGYPT IS COUNTED among the oldest nations on earth. Moses, the writer for the first five books of Scripture, was born in Egypt about fifteen hundred years before Christ. His writings mention Egypt approximately 200 times. The word Pharaoh (or god-king) is mentioned in 129 references in Scripture, with ninety-seven of these being in Moses' writings.

1 The alabaster altar near the entrance to Karnak, watched over by the statues of Amun Ra and the altar builder, Constantine the Great.

2 Three ram-headed sphinxes with accompanying Pharaohs — the ram is the god Knum of the southern area of Egypt.

3 The Shishak Inscription showing Palestinian town names inscribed on the captives' bodies — one of only two places where Israel is mentioned in Egyptian records.

We wondered about the several centuries that the Israelite people spent down in Egypt, much of that time as slaves, and why there were not more records about them. Surely if Moses could write so much about the Egyptians, there should be some records about the Hebrew people. There is a reason: Egyptian historians were forbidden to record any defeats! The gods of Egypt did not allow defeats! This fact is also a very good reason why the fifteenth century BC Israelite migration from Egypt is not recorded in Egyptian writings.

14 Strangely enough, up to the present time among archaeological finds, the Egyptians only mention the Israelites twice. One is the Shishak Inscription found in the Karnak temple complex and the other is found on the Merneptah granite stele in the Cairo Egyptian Museum.

THE KARNAK TEMPLE

Having mentioned the Karnak temple, let's visit it now. The largest ancient temple complex in Egypt is on the north side of the town of Luxor, which has a population today of about 25,000. The temple complex was started around four thousand years ago. We can say that because, at that time, most Pharaohs added their mark to the impressive buildings on the site. The largest of the additions were apparently made by the great builder, Pharaoh Rameses II of the thirteenth century BC. One cannot help but stand in awe at the avenues of ram-headed sphinxes that lead from the Nile river and the Luxor temple to the gateways of the Karnak temple. Under the jaw of each sphinx is a small statue of Rameses II.

Soon after having our tickets clipped at the gates we came across a large statue of the chief of Egyptian gods, Amun Ra. Directly opposite this statue is a much smaller one of Roman Emperor Constantine the Great. Almost between them is an alabaster altar placed there by Constantine. He had converted (at least nominally) to Christianity, for his mother Helena was a Christian. It may be due to his presence at Karnak that some say Constantine had one foot in sun worship and the other in Christianity.

As we moved further on, we viewed the huge hypostyle columns, the sacred lake, thousands of statues including that of Tutankhamun, and Cleopatra's granite needles covered with hieroglyphic inscriptions. The sheer size of the structure not only carves an impression in our minds but fascinates all those who travel along its massive corridors and pathways.

The Shishak Inscription mentioned earlier is found on an inner wall of the

2

Karnak temple alongside an ancient Egyptian calendar. It chronicles the victory of King Shishak over the children of Israel in Palestine at the time of King Rehoboam (1 Kings chapters 12, 14). This archaeological confirmation of

3

1 Boats of all shapes and sizes ply the River Nile carrying passengers and goods.
2 Donkeys prefer a ride on a felucca than to be ridden upon!
3 Fishing on the Nile in the time-honoured way.

Shishak's campaign pictures the god Amun leading rows of captives by a cord. Some of these are undoubtedly Israelites. Altogether there are one hundred and fifty-six captives seen on the relief. On their bodies are inscribed the names of Palestinian towns such as Ajalon, Gibeon and Beth Shan. We are pleased to see this for, as mentioned already, it is only one of two inscriptions to name Israel in Egyptian records extant at the present time. This naturally holds high interest for us as well as among historians, archaeologists and Bible students.

In one corner of the Karnak complex is the sacred lake guarded by another Egyptian god, the Scarab beetle. This scarab was venerated by the ancient Egyptians because they believed it was closely associated with the sun god as creator and sustainer of man's soul in death. It stands on a granite pedestal that is blanketed with hieroglyphic inscriptions.

THE RIVER NILE

Without the Nile meandering its way from Sudan down to its delta and the Mediterranean, Egypt as we know it would not exist. Its waters quench the sandy, thirsty land through multiple irrigation methods, supplying an abundance of fish to millions of Egyptians and providing a waterway used by many vessels for transportation and communication. Where the water stops, the desert begins!

In travelling through the country we noticed several irrigation methods: young women carrying on their heads very heavy clay vessels; the Archimedean screw; blindfolded donkeys turning tread-wheels, the suspended bucket lifting water from one level to another, and occasionally modern pumps either powered from a tractor or independent petrol or diesel powered motors. Each method is employed to lift the water from one level to another and from one area to another. Where there is good irrigation the fertile land brings forth an abundant array of fruits, vegetables and grains. In many areas of the country, irrigation, sowing and reaping are much the same as they were in Bible times. Ploughing is often by oxen and donkeys hitched together. Sowing is carried out by women who throw the grain from a basket or basin. Reaping, particularly of grain, is often by the humble sickle. In contrast,

16

The Nile water continues to make it possible for 50 million Egyptians to have an adequate supply of fruit, vegetables, grains, meats and sugar cane. There has generally been enough water to supply crops for both man and beast. As it has ever been, Egypt is still an agricultural nation. In ancient times, when famines

2

3

neighbours may be using modern tractors with a number of modern implements that are used for irrigation, ploughing, sowing and reaping!

All along the Nile the fishing industry is evident as fishermen ply the waters with their little boats and haul their nets. Once again, in so many cases, there has been little change in their methods over the past two thousand years.

struck neighbouring nations, because of the Nile this land became their bread basket. Genesis 41:57: 'All the countries came to Egypt to buy corn from Joseph, because the famine was severe in all the world.'

HIEROGLYPHICS: THE PICTURE WRITING OF THE EGYPTIANS

For most of the past two thousand years, understanding the hieroglyphics of

ancient Egypt was a forgotten discipline. As a written language it was totally different from the cuneiform writings of the East and from the Hebrew alphabet of Palestine. Greek became a universal language by the time of Christ and even by that time hieroglyphics had been forgotten.

In 1799 the Rosetta stone was found by one of Napoleon's officers. The stone was found near Rosetta, in the Nile delta. The Rosetta stone is one of the popular attractions in the British Museum. On it there is a section of hieroglyphics, a portion of Egyptian demotic script, and another section of Greek. A Frenchman, Jean Champollion, spent arduous hours deciphering the script. The inscription is a decree by Egyptian priests to commemorate the crowning of Ptolemy V Epiphanes, 203-181 BC. Today we are grateful to the genius of Champollion for there are many people who can now read the ancient Egyptian language.

It was in the royal tombs in the Valley of the Kings that we discovered the best preserved and certainly the most

colourful hieroglyphics. One reason for this is that the air is so dry and there is very little humidity. Though hieroglyphic writing to us seems quite primitive, to the ancient Egyptians it conveyed their words in pictures and forms that are now understood by many Egyptologists. In the tombs you can easily recognize the names and even character of the kings, for these are pictured in what is known as a cartouche.

In the tomb of Seti I astrological signs, including animals and men, are depicted

in the 'heavens'. The ancient Egyptians believed the sky contained thirty-six constellations. These, among other stars and the sun in its monthly courses, have been cleverly painted in the ceiling of the tomb of Ramses VI.

RAMSES II
(THE GREAT BUILDER)

We know more about Ramses II of the thirteenth century BC than most other Egyptian kings. This is largely due to his excellent communication and building skills. As we travel from Memphis in the north to Abu Simbel on the border with

1 Traders loading a camel with goods that had just been carried up river by a felucca.

2 A farmer on the West Bank. The method of ploughing has changed very little over the years.

3 The Valley of the Kings — looking down from the Thebian heights down to the tombs of Rameses VI and Tutankhamun.

4 The Rosetta Stone, deciphered by Frenchman Jean Champollion.

Sudan in the south, there are statues, temples, walls, and inscriptions that portray a king who was determined that posterity should remember him. It is truly amazing to see the Rameseum which is not very far from the Valley of the Queens. It is a complex of large buildings containing many pillars and walls in a relatively fair state of preservation. This complex was built in honour of Ramses II. One wall shows the king in combat with the Hittites. Little was known about the Hittites until the turn of the twentieth century. Since that time, at least thirty cities and towns have been discovered in Turkey, the 'home country' of this ancient nation.

While Ramses II was a builder, he, like most pharaohs, was also a destroyer. He desecrated the statues and figures of previous pharaohs and was possibly the person responsible for the destruction of many of Hatshepsut's records, though the person who hated her most was her co-regent Thutmose III. She is the best candidate for the princess who discovered the baby Moses among the papyrus reeds when she went to bathe (Exodus 2:1-6).

20

pile of blocks is that you can go right inside to the very centre where there is a large room containing the empty granite sarcophagus of King Cheops. While the early part of the passage leading to the centre is quite cavernous, at one stage you almost have to crawl on your knees to

4

5

THE PYRAMIDS

Naturally we wanted to see the pyramids. They are truly a spectacular sight. The three large pyramids that stand together at Giza on the western bank of the Nile are just a few kilometres from the centre of Cairo. There are actually more than a hundred pyramids in Egypt, mostly quite small, but some others like the 'Bent' and 'Step' pyramids are much larger and can be seen from Giza. The largest one of all is Cheops' pyramid that covers a land mass of approximately 5 hectares (13 acres). A remarkable thing in this great

make it to the central room. The architecture of the pyramids is certainly quite remarkable and it is not surprising that many wish to see them. Their apex reaches, as it were, right up to the sun, and fits in with the system of worship used by the ancient Egyptians.

1 Visitor's almost need to crawl along the passage inside the Cheops' pyramid that leads up to the sarcophagus. Note the precise fit of the blocks. **2** A side view of the Sphinx gives some idea of its immense size. **3** The impressive entrance to Hatshepsut's temple. She was the daughter of Thutmose I.

MOSES, ISRAEL, EGYPT, AND HATSHEPSUT

We are sure that one of the outstanding mausoleums of the west bank at Luxor is that of Hatshepsut, the daughter of Thutmose I. At the time Moses chose to cast his lot with his own people rather than with the Egyptians, Hatshepsut, his foster mother and the princess, became the Pharaoh after the death of her husband and half-brother, Thutmose II.

3

She was obviously a strong leader and the mausoleum in her honour shows that she was a great builder. Unfortunately, much of the mausoleum and its statuary was destroyed by Thutmose III, who may also have been responsible for her death. She was a co-regent with him during her reign which lasted for twenty-two years. He reigned on until 1450 BC and was probably the pharaoh who went to his death in the Red Sea.

THE PAPYRUS

Egypt was the ancient world's main source of writing materials produced from papyrus reeds. These were plentiful all along the Nile river banks, and especially along the banks of the many branches of the Nile delta. The sheer volume of papyrus reeds makes the following prediction from Isaiah very interesting: Isaiah 19:6, 7, NKJV: ' . . . the brooks of defence will be emptied and dried up; the reeds and rushes will wither. The papyrus reeds by   23 the River (Nile-margin), by the mouth of the River, and everything sown by the River, will wither, be driven away, and be no more.' While there is some papyrus still growing in Egypt it is nothing compared to the vast quantities available for the world in Isaiah's time. Could it be that it disappeared due to the nation's moral decline?

MEMPHIS AND RAMESES II

About an hour south from Cairo by road, travelling past the three main pyramids and along the edge of the desert, we arrive at the famous Step Pyramid. This was a most significant landmark for the necropolis (cemetery) of the ancient city of Memphis. This pyramid was built by the pharaoh Djoser, or rather his architect, Imhotep, in the third dynasty in the third millennium BC. Underneath the surface of the ground near the pyramid are countless tombs. Many are of the king's advisers and their families. In its day Memphis was a very great city but it has been almost lost and there is very little of it to be found today. When we first went out there in 1967, all we were shown was a small museum. On the outside was an alabaster sphinx and inside a huge statue of Rameses II. However, on subsequent visits, after we had contacted local people, we managed to see the remains of some of the temples of old Memphis. It was a very idolatrous city and when you realize that the ancient Egyptians worshipped around two thousand five hundred gods, you can better understand Ezekiel's prophecy: ""'I will destroy the idols and put an end to the images in Memphis.'"" Ezekiel 30:13. It even goes on to say: ""'No longer will there be a prince in Egypt.'""

Since Alexander the Great conquered Egypt, all of the succeeding kings have been foreigners. The last was King Farouk, an Albanian. Amazing how the prophecies have been fulfilled in such careful detail!

3

1 Drawing on papyrus of the dog god Anubis with judgement scales.

2 One of the larger pyramids known as the Step Pyramid is a significant landmark of Memphis.

3 Sarcophagus of the sacred bulls. The lids alone weigh many tons.

4 Sphinx with the head of a man at Memphis.

TUTANKHAMUN AND THE MARVELLOUS TREASURES

When Howard Carter discovered the tomb of Tutankhamun in 1922 it aroused great interest throughout the world. It was the first time that a pharaoh's tomb had been found complete. Tomb robbers over the millennia had left very little of the wealth of other pharaohs for archaeologists to discover. But in this tomb the prized death masks, the jewellery, alabaster vases, gilded wood throne, chariots and three sarcophagi, have all added to an understanding of the wealth inherited by the kings of ancient Egypt.

Tutankhamun was just a boy when he married the daughter of Nefertiti and Ikhnaton. Nefertiti is reputed to have been the most beautiful queen of ancient Egypt. A sculpture of her head and shoulders is to be seen in the Berlin Egyptian museum, which is situated across the road from the Palace of Frederick the Great. Ikhnaton, her pharaoh husband, was probably of Nubian extraction (Nubian Desert of north-east Sudan bordering on Egypt). We deduce this by his facial features and his concern to change the system of worship in Egypt. Ikhnaton moved the palace of the kings from Luxor to Amarna, much nearer to Cairo. Quite a lot of excavation has taken place here, though much of it is once again covered by sand, being located on the edge of the desert. Rock tombs up in the hills behind Amarna and the large temple of Amarna

are well worth visiting. When these were discovered they gave a much clearer picture of this 'different' king who attempted to change the ancient Egyptian system of worshipping many gods to only one god. You can see reliefs of the king worshipping the rays of the sun that were an integral part of his form of worship. There is not much of value at Amarna today. However, from here we can piece together much more about Ikhnaton's young son-in-law, Tutankhamun.

1

1 The bust of beautiful Queen Nefertiti, wife of Ikhnaton and mother-in-law of Tutankhamun.
2 The most famous death-mask of Tutankhamun.

1

Valley of the Kings! This young king was worth millions! However, he was forgotten. Moses gave up this great wealth to be with his people and millions today stand in awe at his courage and faith. (Hebrews 11:23-29.)

2

3

1 Inside the tomb of Tutankhamun showing the sarcophagus and symbolic picture drawings.
2 The death mask that covered the actual mummy of King Tutankhamun.
3 The Colossi of Memnon dwarf the tourists below.
4 The first room of the temple of Rameses II was a holy place, from here the priests entered a most holy place.
5 Wonderful temple of Rameses II carved out of the living rock.

When Howard Carter found the priceless tomb of Tutankhamun, who lived about fifty years after Moses, we could understand better the text of Scripture that says: 'By faith Moses, when he became of age, refused to be called the son of Pharaoh's daughter, choosing rather to suffer affliction with the people of God than to enjoy the passing pleasures of sin, esteeming the reproach of Christ greater riches than the treasures of Egypt; for he looked to the reward.' Hebrews 11:24-26, NKJV.

Millions of people in the Christian, Islamic and Jewish worlds hold Moses in great awe. His faith in God led him to be an outstanding leader and spiritual father of the Israelite nation. Riches never got the better of him. His name has been etched indelibly on history. On the other hand, nobody knew about Tutankhamun until Howard Carter found his statue in the Karnak temple complex and then later discovered his golden tomb in the

28

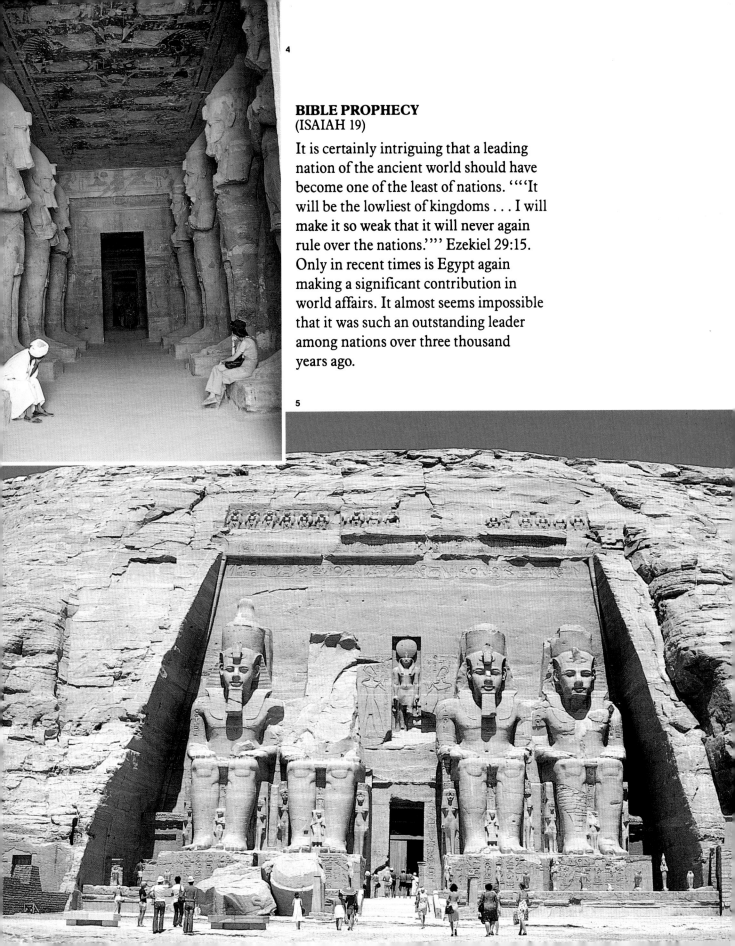

BIBLE PROPHECY
(ISAIAH 19)

It is certainly intriguing that a leading nation of the ancient world should have become one of the least of nations. ""It will be the lowliest of kingdoms . . . I will make it so weak that it will never again rule over the nations."" Ezekiel 29:15. Only in recent times is Egypt again making a significant contribution in world affairs. It almost seems impossible that it was such an outstanding leader among nations over three thousand years ago.

5

Iran

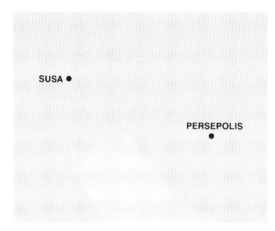

Persian empire under Cyrus. His tomb is to be seen near Susa, where one can see the Persian palace made famous by Queen Esther. Daniel is revered by Jew, Christian and Muslim alike, and because of his writings he has been called 'the greatest of the prophets'. Of all the prophets quoted, Daniel's name is the only one mentioned by Jesus Christ in the gospels (Matthew 24:15).

PERSEPOLIS

When the last Shah of Iran (Pavlavi) ruled in Tehran, he held a spectacular festival at Persepolis commemorating the

DANIEL AND THE KINGS OF PERSIA

IN THE SECTION on Iraq we noted that Daniel was taken captive by Nebuchadnezzar II. He was still living when King Cyrus wrested Babylon from Belshazzar, the son of Nabonidus. Daniel was also made a prime minister of the

1 On the streets of Shiraz in Iran melons and beans sell for a fraction of the asking price in the West.   2 Persepolis is the best preserved of the four palaces used by the Persian rulers. Depicted on this stone column is Darius fighting the beast, possibly representing the Devil.   3 In front of steps leading up to the Persepolis palace are bas-reliefs depicting the Medes and Persians. The pillared audience hall was 65 metres (200 feet) long and 20 metres (65 feet) high.

two-thousand-year reign of the Persian kings. We were amazed at the size and preservation of Persepolis which is the best preserved of the four palaces used by the ancient Persian rulers. We now travel four and a half miles north of Persepolis to Naqsh-i-Rustum. Here is the valley of the tombs made for many of the Persian kings. The largest tomb is that of Darius the Great. In a field nearby some

bedouins have camped. It is unusual for us to see that the floors of their tents are covered with Persian carpets. Most of us cannot afford such luxuries! About thirty miles north at Pasargadae is the tomb of Cyrus the Great who was responsible for capturing Babylon.

BEHISTUN ROCK

One of the great feats of archaeology was the time Henry Rawlinson climbed a very high rickety ladder held by a young soldier, to take impressions of the Behistun Rock inscription. This was back in 1835-39. The rock inscriptions

were fully deciphered by 1855 and an astonished Western World discovered that ancient cuneiform writing could now be understood for the first time. Like the Rosetta stone, the inscriptions were also in three languages, Old Persian, Elamite and Babylonian. Some people questioned the veracity of Rawlinson's work. When Ashurbanipal's library was discovered at Nineveh in 1853 and, as a result of Rawlinson's work, many tablets were translated, he was vindicated.

1 Cut out of the rock face below his tomb Darius is depicted on horseback with a captive monarch pleading for his life.

2 The Valley of the Kings, north of Persepolis, Persia. The tomb of Darius the Great is on the right.

Syria

TELL MARDIKH AND EBLA

TWO THOUSAND YEARS before Christ, the kings of Ebla went to war with surrounding nations and in peaceful times traded with them. Their centre was close to the modern-day 'Beehive' village of Mardikh. Since 1964 an Italian archaeological team directed by Professor Paolo Matthiae of the University of Rome began digging at the magnificent Tell Mardikh that covered about 56 hectares (140 acres). Over the years the excavations continued. The Italians not only established the position of the gates of the city, but most important of all, they found the king's palace. It was here that in 1974 forty-two cuneiform tablets were found. Then in 1975 the world heard about the discovery of a whole library containing approximately 15,000 articles and letters on clay tablets. By 1978 more

1 Typical traditional beehive homes of northern Syria.

2 Archaeological excavations of Tel Mardikh with metre-wide separations between sections — this method was first used by Kathleen Kenyon the famous British archaeologist.

tablets had been found and the total amounted to around 20,000. Much of the work of deciphering was left to Professor Pettinato. Many problems arose between the two main archaeologists, and also between them and the Syrian government. These obstacles have delayed translation considerably. However, according to Professor

33

1

2

Pettinato, the tablets do mention that trading took place between Ebla and Sodom and Gomorrah and the other cities of the plain mentioned in Genesis 14.

RAS SHAMRA

One of the most important cuneiform discoveries was at Ras Shamra in Syria. These tablets go back to 1400 BC. They give a clear picture of the Canaanite gods and goddesses, their temples and the religious rites performed in them, including prayers and hymns. It is interesting that many of their hymns were not unlike those used by the Israelites in later years. These Ugarit tablets have shown many similarities in religious rites to those of the Israelites.

DAMASCUS AND PAUL

Damascus as a capital city and provincial town was also a walled city. It is mentioned forty-five times in the

3

have made a very beautiful mausoleum for what they believe is his body. It is to a tall minaret from the same mosque that it is claimed Christ will come when He returns.

WATER WHEELS OF HAMA

Leaving Damascus we travelled in our minibus to the interesting city of Hama. Like Damascus, Hama or Hamath

1 Excavations at Ras Shamra in Syria uncovered information concerning the many gods of the Canaanites.

2 Old wall of Damascus. The city dates back to the time of Abraham, and is where Paul was converted.

scriptures and was a strong city in the time of Abraham. This patriarch's servant was called Eliezer of Damascus. Damascus gained fame in New Testament times when Paul converted before entering the city. He was taken to the home of Ananias who baptized him into Christ. Instead of persecuting Christians, Paul began to preach Christ in the synagogues. However, his life was now under threat and so he was let down the wall in a basket (Acts 9:25). Naturally we wanted to see this ancient city which is also the capital of modern-day Syria. The bazaar here is one of the largest in the Middle East. Here we saw bartering on many luxury items from Rolls Royce cars to second-hand Persian carpets — and on day-to-day necessities such as vegetables and fruits. Things have not changed much in Damascus except, perhaps, the goods on sale. . . .

In the main mosque the Muslims claim to have the body of John the Baptist. They

1 A weaver at work in the market place of Damascus.

2 The water wheels of Hama date from Roman times and were used to lift water to the aqueduct for irrigation.

3 Paul was taken to the street called Straight to the home of Ananias.

4 Present-day Shechem from the 4,000-year-old walls of ancient Shechem nestled below Mount Gerizim, the mount of blessings.

3

1

(biblical name) is very old and is mentioned in Scripture about fifty-five times. It mainly comes into the war scenes of Scripture but is also a geographical location for measuring distances. The famous water wheels are from Roman times and were used to lift water to an aqueduct. It was fascinating to see some teenagers carried up by the huge water wheels and diving back into the river at just the right time. Through these wheels agricultural land could be irrigated and nearby villages replenished with the waters from the river.

2

Israel

SHECHEM

ARCHAEOLOGIST G. ERNEST WRIGHT first
began excavating at Shechem in 1956.
When Abraham left Ur of the Chaldees,
his household and animals moved
along the fertile valleys of the Euphrates
and Tigris rivers to Haran. He then
stopped until His father died and was
buried in this place. Some relatives
stayed in the area as we read later in the

4

book of Genesis. Eventually Abraham
and his family arrived in Canaan and
settled for a time in Shechem. (Genesis
12:1-6.)

Over the years since Wright's excavation,
there has been considerable
archaeological activity at Shechem. Not
only was it famous in Abraham's time but
in Gideon's too. Then it was the centre
for the short-lived reign of Abimelech,
Gideon's son. After the death of Solomon
it was where Rehoboam brought the
tribes who wanted him as king and where
he was crowned. It also became the
capital of the Northern kingdom of
Israel. It is close to Jacob's well — a
mecca for tourists today even as it was in
the days of Jesus (John 4). Towering up
from Shechem and Jacob's well are the
two mountains known as Gerizim and
Ebal, the mountains of blessings and
cursings.

37

2   1

3

AHAB'S IVORY PALACE AND IVORIES

Several kilometres to the north of
Shechem the foundations of buildings
and palace walls of the kings of Israel
have been discovered. This is at Sebastyeh
in Samaria. After King Solomon's reign
the twelve tribes divided into two nations,
Judah and Israel. The tribes of Judah and
Benjamin made up the people and the
territories for the kings of Judah in the
south. In the north the other ten tribes of
Israel resided and worshipped on Mount
Gerizim. Today the Samaritans still
worship there and offer yearly sacrifices.

King Ahab, a later king of Israel, married
Jezebel, the daughter of King Ethbaal
the king of the Sidonians in Lebanon
(1 Kings 16:31). She brought with her
the prophets of Baal. Very soon Baal
worship had invaded the kingdom of
the ten tribes of Israel. This probably

contributed to the wicked reign of the king that lasted for twenty-two years (1 Kings 16:29, 30.)

Ahab imported ivories from all over the world and his palace became known as the Ivory house (1 Kings 22:39, NKJV). Strangely enough, the critics of Scripture considered this text to be a fable. How could Ahab have had an ivory house? He had evidently lined some of the rooms of his palace with imported ivories. It is interesting to go to the British Museum and see a number of these ivories. Many were taken into the Assyrian palaces when the Assyrian kings destroyed Samaria and took captive a large number of the Israelites from the north. When Layard and other archaeologists excavated Nineveh they found many of these ivories which had been in Ahab's ivory house. Again the critics have been silenced!

DEAD SEA CAVES

It was an exciting time for us in 1967

1 An amphitheatre near Ahab's palace at Sebastyeh (Samaria).
2, 3 Ivories from Ahab's 'house of ivory'; a sign of luxury.
4, 5 In/on the Dead Sea! Too much salt within is dangerous, but plenty of salt without supports the body.

4

5

when we first visited the Dead Sea caves and the nearby ruins of Qumran. The secrets of Qumran and its many treasures began to be unravelled in 1947 at the finding of the Dead Sea caves. The greatest of these were in the many parchment scrolls found in jars. These

became the earliest manuscripts discovered to date of some Old Testament books of the Bible. Five scrolls comprising parts of the book of Isaiah and even more of Daniel were discovered. Carbon dating methods generally place these manuscripts up to 150 years before Christ. Until the time of this wonderful discovery, the oldest manuscripts of these scriptural books were approximately one thousand years later. Many critics were silenced with the translation of these scrolls. For example: the book of Isaiah was thought to be written after Christ and not by the eighth century BC prophet. However, with this find it is now generally believed that Isaiah was indeed written by the prophet. Daniel also was believed to have been a contemporary of Christ or written in the late Maccabean period. However, many scholars now consider that the book belongs to the great prophet of the times of King Nebuchadnezzar II and Cyrus the Great.

MASADA

When Jerusalem was finally burned and ransacked by the Romans in AD 70, they continued their rampage over the land against the Jewish strongholds. The Herodion outside Bethlehem fell, as did Macchaerus, north of Kerak. Then the Roman armies stormed down to Masada which rises 304 metres (1,000 feet) near the Dead Sea. Because it was built on a plateau above

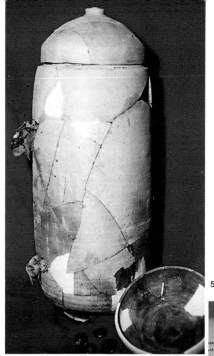

1 Cave IV, which held a vast number of manuscript fragments a thousand years older than any previously known!

2 Mushroom-shaped salt formations in the shallows of the Dead Sea.

3 The Qumran ruins on the western shore of the Dead Sea where the Essenes copied much of the Old Testament Scriptures.

4 The great ramp built by the Romans in order to capture the fortress of Masada.

5
6

4

5 One of the jars that contained the valuable scrolls.

6 The Isaiah Scroll, part of 'the greatest manuscript discovery of modern times'.

41

2

1

precipitous cliffs it took the Romans until
AD 73 to destroy it. They did this by
building a large ramp, and making a
covering for their battering ram to stop
the hail of stones and arrows from killing
the soldiers. Inch by inch the ramp was
built and the battering ram placed in
position. When the Romans finally broke
through the massive wall there were only

had just passed Bethany, rounded yet another corner and — there it was, the old walls of Jerusalem, with the Dome of the Rock peeping over the top. Like many before us, our emotions took over for a minute or two. Even though we have been back a number of times, we never get weary of tramping around this remarkable old city.

Archaeology has been responsible for the discovery of many Old Testament sites in Jerusalem. Among them is Hezekiah's tunnel, built to take water from the spring Gihon (outside the city walls) into the Pool of Siloam. In 2 Samuel 5 and 1 Chronicles 11:4-9 we find the interesting story of David's general, Joab. He entered into the city by stealth and opened the gates for David's armies. He

1 Looking out on to the Dead Sea from the heights of Masada.
2 Mount Masada — the plateau-topped rock on which Herod built his famous fortress.
3 The Dome of the Rock, built over the traditional site of Abraham's test of faith on Mount Moriah.

about six people left. They told the horrendous story of mass suicide and the burning of stores of food and clothing. This was the last stronghold of the Jews.

JERUSALEM

We can still remember the first time we saw the old city of Jerusalem. We were in a service taxi coming from Jordan. We

3

1

2

did so from a shaft that went up from an earlier tunnel into the city. (See Kathleen M. Kenyon, *Archaeology in the Holy Land*, fourth edition, page 235.) It was up this shaft that water could be hauled by way of leather water vessels. It wasn't until the time of King Hezekiah that the tunnel was finished and the water taken into the pool of Siloam.

In 1880 an inscription was found in the tunnel by some young boys. The inscription tells how the tunnel was made

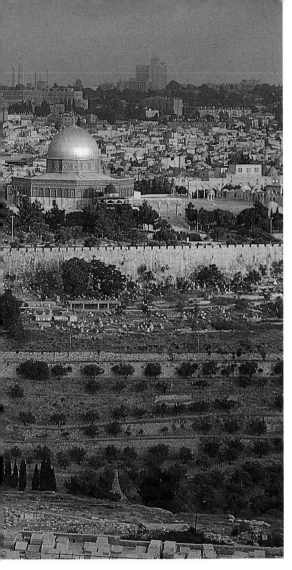

Warren. These expose many great stones placed there by Herod's men. In more recent times the white marble stairs leading to the temple area have been excavated. Near them are many water pools where perhaps the early Christians were baptized (Acts 2). It is hard to excavate the temple area these days because of the buildings now standing

1 The eastern wall of the old city of Jerusalem and the Dome of the Rock where Solomon's magnificent temple once stood.
2 Here Hezekiah's tunnel delivers water from the spring Gihon into the pool of Siloam.
3 Jerusalem's wailing wall which is largely constructed from the foundations of Herod's temple.

3

and its depth under the surface of the hill. Today this inscription may be seen in the Istanbul archaeological museum.

Nobody can be *exactly* sure where Solomon's temple was located. When King Herod rebuilt the temple and its foundations, he used large blocks of stone that are easy for us to identify because of their design. Those stones can today be seen at the western (or wailing) wall. In the synagogue section one can see some large shafts dug around 1867 by Charles

1 Capernaum's white limestone synagogue with an elaborate entrance facing Jerusalem.
2 Sunset across the Sea of Galilee.

there and the religious bans by Muslims and Christians alike.

In the late 1980s Israeli archaeologists found a number of the earliest buildings from the time of Solomon, including a gate house and even one or two of the gates of the early walls.

CAPERNAUM

Jesus spent most of His ministry around the Lake of Galilee, as predicted in Isaiah 9:1, 2. This country setting is a delightful place to visit and to stay for a day or two. One cannot help but visit old Capernaum. The most notable building reconstructed here is the ancient synagogue, built on the ruins of the synagogue where Jesus preached on the Sabbath (Mark 1:21). Nearby was the house of Peter's mother-in-law (verse 29). Here also is a stone relief of the ark of the covenant on wheels, representing the time that it was returned from the Philistines (2 Samuel 6:3).

1

2

CAESAREA

From Capernaum we travelled by car over the mountains to the coast and down to Caesarea. For many years this was the army base for the Roman soldiers. It is the only place, apart from the Scriptures, where the name Pilate is to be found. His name is chiselled on a small pillar of stone. He was the Roman proconsul responsible for allowing Christ to be

3

1

2

1 This aqueduct brought fresh water into the city of Caesarea from the springs beneath Mount Carmel, 21 kilometres (13 miles) away.

2 Pilate's name was inscribed on this stone which was found at Caesarea in 1961. The stone may have recorded the building of a shrine in honour of Emperor Tiberius.

3 Ruins of the gate at Caesarea. Built in grand style it was the base from which the Romans administered Palestine.

crucified. Besides this, Caesarea has yielded many treasures including buildings. The most famous being the amphitheatre. This has been beautifully restored by the Israelis and is often used for concerts and plays on some of the balmy evenings for which Israel is famous.

It was to the area of Caesarea that King Hiram of Lebanon floated the cedar logs for Solomon's temple and home. From here these massive logs were hauled overland to Jerusalem. It was here also in New Testament times that Paul came and testified of his faith to Felix, Festus and Agrippa, and made an appeal to be judged by Caesar in Rome.

47

Lebanon

WHAT A MAGNIFICENT COUNTRY — literally the 'emerald' of the Middle East! Its lush countryside and geographical position have been the envy of countless nations over the years. It is a country that was always a pleasure to travel in. The exception has been the recent times of civil war that have devastated the country financially, physically and morally. The beautiful city of Beirut — noted for its wonderful French architecture — has been badly crippled. This country, the paradise of the East, the banking centre of the Arab world, has almost lost its heart. No doubt it will rise again to prominence out of its destruction and ashes.

BEIRUT
BYBLOS
BAALBEK
SIDON
TYRE

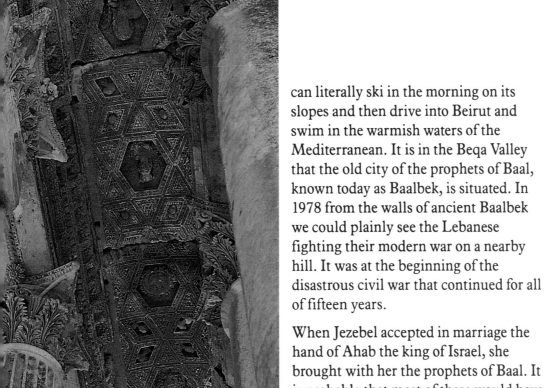

2

1 Stairway leading into
the temple of Baachus at
Baalbek and its famous
banqueting hall.
2 The fluted columns
with their intricately
carved capitals and
ceiling of the temple of
Baachus.

BAALBEK

Climbing out of Beirut over its curving, mountainous road, we eventually drive down into the picturesque Beqa Valley. This very fertile valley of reddish soil is literally the 'bread basket' of Lebanon. As we drive past the many orchards and productive fields we get an excellent view of the highest mountain in the Middle East, Mount Hermon. In the winter one can literally ski in the morning on its slopes and then drive into Beirut and swim in the warmish waters of the Mediterranean. It is in the Beqa Valley that the old city of the prophets of Baal, known today as Baalbek, is situated. In 1978 from the walls of ancient Baalbek we could plainly see the Lebanese fighting their modern war on a nearby hill. It was at the beginning of the disastrous civil war that continued for all of fifteen years.

When Jezebel accepted in marriage the hand of Ahab the king of Israel, she brought with her the prophets of Baal. It is probable that most of these would have been trained at a place like Baalbek. Mark Twain was once asked why he called the horse he was riding Baalbek. He replied, 'It is such a magnificent ruin.' I am not sure about the horse, but at least the old city is indeed a magnificent ruin.

Not far from the city is a quarry where the ancient Lebanese carved out the limestone pillars for their temples. Inside the city there are six massive pillars of the temple of Jupiter still standing. This whole temple must have approached the grandeur of Solomon's Temple in Jerusalem, even though it was built about a millennium later in the first century AD. The water spouts around the roof structure had been carved in the form of lions' mouths. Alongside these splendidly crafted spouts is filigree work that was obviously executed by skilled craftsmen. The inverted swastika (sign of eternity) and the egg and dart (signs of

49

1

3

2

An impressive arena is where the high altar still stands. Sacrifices were made on this to the sun god Jupiter, and to his son Bacchus. Throughout the Middle East, the system of Babylonian worship has been discovered. Nimrod, Ishtar and Tamuz made up the Babylonian counterfeit trinity. They reappeared as Jupiter, Semiramus and Bacchus (Baal) or as Zeus, Diana and Baal — and other names. It depended in which country or province the worshippers lived.

It is now possible to understand better some reasons why Baal worship and the religious system of Babylon were both severely condemned by the prophets of the Old Testament. Spiritual Babylon was to come to its end as described in the book of Revelation.

sex worship and immorality) are to be seen with very little decay considering the period of time since the structure was built.

Next door is the temple of Bacchus. Bacchus was the supposed son of Jupiter. Again there are many limestone columns, but this time much smaller. The workmanship here is superb.

50

4

BYBLOS

Lebanon has been the centre of many a bloody battle from the times of the Egyptians, Assyrians and Babylonians right down to the present. At the Dog river is a very ancient bridge over which many armies of nations fought and conquered or were defeated. If a nation was victorious at this point then mostly on the south side of the river was inscribed in the rock face a relief reminding posterity of the victory. One can still be seen chiselled in the north side rock from the times of King Nebuchadnezzar II of Babylon, and that was 2,500 years ago!

Today on the north side of the river is a magnificent statue of Christ. It is easily seen on the cliff face as one travels along the coast road to the ancient Phoenician town of Byblos. Here they grew an

1 The steps leading up into the temple of Saturn at Baalbek.
2 Statue of Baal.   3 The high altar in the temple of Bacchus where sacrifices were made to the sun god Jupiter.   4 The statue of Christ with outstretched arms looks over the Dog river.   5 The old bridge over the Dog river — the battle ground where the destiny of many nations was decided.

5

abundance of papyrus reed for export, after the industry in Egypt had collapsed (Isaiah 19:6, 7, NKJV). Byblos literally gave the Scriptures their title of 'Bible'. The Greek word Byblos, the Book, was given to the reeds as they were mashed, glued and then written upon! The Scriptures are literally the Book of books.

The ancient Canaanites had a centre in Byblos and the remains of their temple may still be seen. There is a small natural harbour here today. This was one of the places from which the cedars of Lebanon were floated down to the area of Caesarea to Hiram, king of Tyre and friend of King Solomon. He assisted in the building of King Solomon's temple and house by sending him both the precious cedar wood and craftsmen to fashion the timbers (1 Kings 9:10-14).

On their way to attempt to free Jerusalem from the Muslims, the Crusaders built a castle here which is still in relatively good condition. It overlooks the old town of Byblos including its Roman ruins of nearly two thousand years ago.

SIDON

Travelling south from Beirut let us take you to the ancient city of Sidon. We are following a similar route over which Alexander the Great in the fourth century BC rode his trusty steed. When he arrived at Sidon he was appalled at the horrific sight. The whole population had joined in mass suicide — men, women and children. Only a handful were left.

Two hundred years before Alexander the prophet Ezekiel had declared that this would happen in Sidon. Notice Ezekiel 28:22, 23: "''This is what the Sovereign Lord says: "I am against you, O Sidon, and I will gain glory within you. They

2

The population knew that this successful young ruler was on his way. They decided against being taken as slaves as their ancestors had been two hundred years before under Babylon's Nebuchadnezzar II. They opted for suicide. The prophet had it right!

TYRE

will know that I am the Lord, when I inflict punishment on her and show myself holy within her. I will send a plague upon her and make blood flow in her streets. The slain will fall within her, with the sword against her on every side. Then they will know that I am the Lord."'''''

When Alexander marched past Sidon he eventually came to the Phoenician city of Tyre. The old city was still in ruins left by Nebuchadnezzar. The Phoenicians had a large merchant navy that visited every port in the Mediterranean and reached as far as England. These boats were their strength. When Nebuchadnezzar II had

3

come upon their city, while he destroyed the buildings, the people had gone out to the Island of Tyre just half a mile from the shore. The Babylonians had no ships and the people were safe. The prophets had declared that Tyre would be destroyed by Nebuchadnezzar (Ezekiel 26:7-9). However, other nations would come against her (verse 3). They did! When Alexander came against Tyre he finished off the work that

Nebuchadnezzar had started many years before. He took all the bricks, timber, pottery and soil of Old Tyre and laid them in the sea. While the Phoenicians had their boats, Alexander had men. He used them and made a large causeway out to the Island. His soldiers were then able to capture Tyre island.

The prophet Ezekiel proclaimed two hundred and fifty years earlier (Ezekiel

1

26:12-14): "'They will plunder your wealth and loot your merchandise; they will break down your walls and demolish your fine houses and throw your stones, timber and rubble into the sea. I will put an end to your noisy songs, and the music of your harps will be heard no more. I will make you a bare rock, and you will become a place to spread fishing nets. You will never be rebuilt, for I the Lord have spoken, declares the Sovereign Lord.'" The truth lies in Ezekiel 26:21: "'I will bring you to a horrible end and you will be no more. You will be sought, but you will never again be found, declares the Sovereign Lord.'" The original city on the mainland has never been found.

Tyre island still boasts a strong population that has often been bombed by the Israelis because of their belief that PLO officers have worked from Tyre against Israel. Perhaps a fresh water spring may give a little clue to the original city's whereabouts.

On what may have been the old city of Tyre I have noticed the local fishermen drying and mending their nets. It is desolate. This great city of yesteryear has come to naught.

The gospel writers, Matthew, Mark, Luke and John, all wrote about the cross. It was designed by the Phoenicians 700 years before. The design was to give the maximum torture for the minimum of unconsciousness. It was a cruel death. In those early days it was designed not only as a punishment but as a sacrifice to the sun god worshipped by most ancient religions. This form of punishment was used by the Romans. The fact that Christ died on the cross within hours was most unusual. Mark 15:44, 45, 'Pilate was surprised to hear that he was already

1 Columns in the sea from old Tyre which were probably dumped there by Alexander the Great.

2 Fishermen dragging in their nets near old Tyre.

dead. Summoning the centurion, he asked him if Jesus had already died. When he learned from the centurion that it was so, he gave the body to Joseph.' Pilate was surprised for even when nailed to crosses, victims lasted for up to three or five days. If tied, they might last up to two weeks.

The cross generally had a little horn or seat that took the weight off the body. This was created to stop the victim's body from collapsing. Crucifixion was very cruel and yet it tells us something about those early Phoenicians who were almost annihilated by Alexander the Great.

1 Cool greens in the Garden of Gethsemane and a view over the Kidron Valley to the Golden Gate.

2 An ancient rock-hewn tomb in Jerusalem in a garden setting similar to that where Jesus was buried.

3 A glimpse of the Treasury through the narrow gorge, the Siq, entrance into Petra.

Jordan

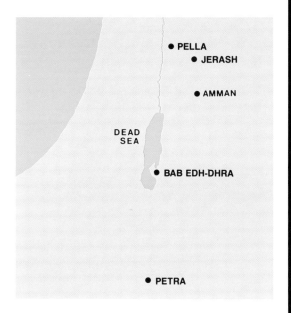

PETRA

WE VISITED ONE of the most fascinating places of the Middle East. The poet Burgon called this place 'Rose red Petra, half as old as time'. The first inhabitants were the Edomites or the children of Esau. They were finally slain at the time of King Amaziah of Israel. The city was discovered in recent times by a Swiss explorer named Burckhardt employed by the British Museum for this purpose. His expertise in both Arabic and the geography of the Middle East made it likely that he might find this hidden mysterious city.

His heart must have beat faster as he viewed for the first time the marvellous

3

Treasury building or El Khazneh. To get there we left the modern hotel and police station. It seemed that a hundred young Arabs were wanting us to ride their horses. It is fun to ride a horse so we opted for this alternative to wearing out our shoes on the stony track. For one-and-a-half kilometres (over a mile) our horses took us through a canyon with cliffs reaching up to 61 metres (200 feet) above the valley floor to the sky, which was a magnificent blue. Then through a bend in the pathway we saw what Burckhardt saw — the Treasury. During the day its natural façade reflects different colours from pink to purple and brown. It was literally carved out of the cliff face and is one of several impressive temples and buildings in this unique valley.

Thousands of homes have been discovered. It was obviously a very well kept and well positioned city. It was ideal for caravan routes travelling from Arabia and up through the fertile crescent to Syria, Lebanon and Mesopotamia. Side routes took the caravans to Israel.

1
2

3

1 The one-and-a-half-kilometre (mile-long), 61-metre (200-foot) deep Siq through which travellers enter Petra is seen opposite the Treasury door.

2 High up above Petra is the place of sacrifice where both animal and human sacrifices were offered.

3 Petra, being situated on the lucrative spice route from India to the Mediterranean, gave the Nabatean's who lived in these rock-hewn homes of their capital immense power in the east-west trade.

4 The Treasury or El Khaznah carved from the living rock.

While the Edomites were cousins to the Israelites, on the journey from Egypt the Israelites were forbidden to traverse the soil of Edom and so took the longer route around them and through Moab to the north. Eventually the Edomites were mostly killed by king Amaziah. It was the Nabateans who built most of the temples, homes and palaces in Petra. King Herod the Great was half Nabatean and half Israelite.

2

1

JERASH

The biblical city of Gerasa became one of the cities of the Decapolis in New Testament times. To get there, we left Amman and travelled on the road towards Syria. There are many valleys and orchards on the way. Eventually the road winds down to a small gorge through which flows the brook Jabbok (Genesis 32:22, 23). Only a few kilometres and we are at Jerash with its imposing entrance gate. The best preserved building in this old city is the Amphitheatre which is still used on occasions by the Jordanians.

From the heights of the Amphitheatre one can see the market square and the main streets that lead past many old bazaars and temples. In the first century a church was built here and a large baptistery in which at least twenty people

high security region for the Jordanian army and special permission has had to be obtained to go down to these famous archaeological finds. The road is quite steep and there are many horseshoe bends. The area is particularly desolate but at Bab Edh-Dhra there was discovered white-hot ash. When we first visited the site in 1978, we dug into this ash with our bare hands and discovered a large piece of pottery. The ash is quite

3

1 Steps leading into the temple complex at Gerasa, modern-day Jerash, one of the ten towns of the Decapolis. 2 The amphitheatre has perfect acoustics enabling orators to be heard wherever people sit. 3 Ancient Gerasa has s Greek-style chequer-board street plan. At the end of a long colonnaded street is the circular market place.

could be baptized by immersion at one time.

BAB EDH-DHRA

One of the exciting finds in Jordan in recent times has been the buried village of Bab Edh-Dhra. For years there have been stories of the sighting of Sodom and Gomorrah below the surface of the Dead Sea. Some of the first were made by pilots in fighter aircraft flying over the region. However, Israeli divers have failed to find any buried cities.

Sitting on a high ridge south of the capital, Amman in Jordan, is the crusader castle of Kerak. Today a part of this is used as a museum for discoveries made in the Bab Edh-Dhra region. Travelling from Kerak down to the Dead Sea region has been somewhat difficult. It has been a

soft even today, and has been dated back to the time of Sodom and Gomorrah. It is remarkable that when many people considered these cities and other cities of

1 Circular burial houses discovered at Bab edh-Dhra the possible site of Sodom. They are an indication that the construction of these charnal-houses points to a wealthy population.

2 Foundations of buildings at Bab edh-Dhra, believed to be the city of Sodom.

3 The temple and administrative area of Pella located east of the Jordan river, and one of the cities of the Decapolis.

the plain to be legendary, the Bible mentions them in many places, and Jesus Himself mentions them as having existed. (Genesis 19:24-29; Matthew 11:23, 24.)

Today many archaeologists and Bible students are convinced that these cities have been found. They belong to Abraham's time and have suffered intense burning. The cities of the plain mentioned in Genesis 14 may well be the cities of the Jordan Valley so recently discovered.

PELLA (AT ONE TIME IN SYRIA)

We had always hoped to visit Pella. When Christ mentioned in Matthew 24:20, "'Pray that your flight will not take place in winter or on the Sabbath'", many Christians must have wondered to where they could flee. Nearly forty years later when the Roman armies surrounding Jerusalem temporarily withdrew to their barracks at Caesarea (AD 66) the Christians fled across the Jordan to Pella. Today it can be visited in the very north-western section of Jordan, close to the Syrian border. The road that is easiest to take winds northward on the east bank of the Jordan through some of the most fertile of Jordanian country.

Pella was not a large settlement but there are some very well laid out homes, and a very attractive temple. Christians were evidently quite safe here and missed the holocaust of AD 70 when Jerusalem was gutted by the Romans under their general Titus. The Christians indeed had their prayers answered!

Turkey

THE SEVEN CHURCHES

THE LAST BOOK of the Scriptures contains letters and messages to the seven churches of the Roman province of Asia (Asia Minor or Turkey, as we know it today). These were not the only Christian churches in Asia Minor. There were also churches at Colossae, Antioch, Iconium, Lystra and Derbe, to name a few. However, these seven churches were not only in close proximity, being on the Roman highway, but they contained different characteristics that are also apparent in periods of church history to the present time. Many theologians are agreed that the letters have a fourfold application: 1. A message to the local church in the city that bears the church's name; 2. A message to the city itself; 3. A message for a period of time in the history of the Christian Church; and 4. A message to each individual in the Christian Church, either at the time of writing or even today. So we decided to travel down the Roman road to visit these churches and the towns which gave them their names.

EPHESUS

Ephesus is the first letter. When the prophet John was writing this letter, there was a thriving tourist trade in Ephesus. People would travel from all over the Mediterranean to come to this city. They more often than not came by boat and could land at its harbour at the mouth of the Cayster river.

Ephesus means 'desirable'. It was pleasantly situated at the beginning of the Roman highway which wound its way through Asia Minor. The climate was very congenial and allowed an abundance of fruits and vegetables. It boasted a very large temple in honour of the multi-breasted goddess Diana. Tourists could buy little statues of Diana made by the local silversmiths. Her temple was about four times larger than the Parthenon in Athens. Today one can hardly find the ruins — though statues of the goddess are to be found in the museum of Seljuk, a nearby bustling town.

Ephesus flaunts a large well preserved amphitheatre. There are also a number of small temples, a famous market place

63

(agora), a rebuilt library, harbour installations (though today the sea is miles away), and marble-lined shops that lead up a steep incline from the agora towards the final home of Mary, the mother of Christ. (Tradition says that John brought her to this pastorate some time after the crucifixion.)

Located beside the museum at nearby Seljuk is a first-century church of John, a baptistery where baptism was performed by immersion, and the traditional grave of John. In the museum of Seljuk are two well-preserved statues of the goddess Diana. She was known as the 'mother of God' and it was in her honour that the silversmiths of Ephesus made little images and a reasonable living. No wonder they were not impressed with the preaching of Paul — their very livelihood was at stake!

Let's capture some of the message of

1 One of the many statues of Artemis or Diana, goddess of wild animals, hunting and the moon. The silversmiths as Ephesus made small models of her for pilgrims to take home. 2 The Great Theatre of Ephesus with its sixty-six tiers of stone seats, and the colonnaded road that once led to the harbour. During Paul's visit this was the scene of a riot. 3 A detail of the Library of Celsus, Ephesus. 4 Ephesus is the greatest archaeological site of all. This mosaic pavement is off Curetes Street.

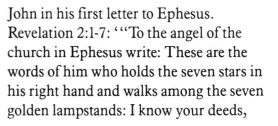

John in his first letter to Ephesus. Revelation 2:1-7: '"To the angel of the church in Ephesus write: These are the words of him who holds the seven stars in his right hand and walks among the seven golden lampstands: I know your deeds, your hard work and your perseverance. I know that you cannot tolerate wicked men, that you have tested those who claim to be apostles but are not, and have found them false. You have persevered and have endured hardships for my name, and have not grown weary.

"Yet I hold this against you: you have forsaken your first love. Remember the height from which you have fallen! Repent and do the things you did at first. If you do not repent I will come to you and remove your lampstand from its place. But you have this in your favour: You hate the practices of the Nicolaitans, which I also hate.

"He who has an ear, let him hear what the Spirit says to the churches. To him who overcomes, I will give the right to eat from the tree of life, which is in the paradise of God.'"

In the heart of Ephesus was the magnificent Temple of Diana. In stark contrast was a humble Christian church — greatly extended in the first century and even more so at a later date. The members had forgotten their *first love*. I think you can see why some theologians suggest that this and the other six letters have a fourfold application. Not only to the church and local city, but in this case to the first period of the Christian Church from, say, AD 33 until the end of the first century. Probably soon after John wrote this book. But there is something about this letter that seems to speak to every person of every age. Very

1

personal — for it sadly seems such a normal experience for us to lose our first love to God and also to man.

Ephesus is well worth a visit and many tourists go there every year. I wonder if they look beyond the amazing ruins to the appeal in John's letter!

1 Entrance into the Church of John at Seljuk.

2 The reconstructed Library of Celsus at Ephesus.

2

1

SMYRNA

Our next port of call was about sixty miles away. To get there we travelled on a new motorway up the coast for about an hour and came to Izmir (the modern name Izmir reflects the ancient Smyrna. Today its sparse ruins are to be found nestled in the heart of the thriving city. Its market place had some buildings that were three storeys high. Well built, it has survived some terrible earthquakes down

through the years. Even John spoke about the tribulation this city and the church would have to go through. Revelation 2:9, 10: '''I know your afflictions and your poverty — yet you are rich! I know the slander of those who say they are Jews and are not, but are a synagogue of Satan. Do not be afraid of what you are about to suffer. I tell you, the devil will put some of you in prison to test you, and you will suffer persecution for ten days. Be faithful, even to the point of death, and I will give you the crown of life.''' Notice that there is no reproof to this city. In Church history it probably represents the second and third centuries of the Christian era when the Church began its major period of growth, yet at the same time struggled with a lot of persecution. The hills around the city are curiously shaped like a crown. The promised blessing in the text fits well into the vocabulary of the locals!

2

PERGAMOS

Travelling north and leaving the coast for a few miles, we arrived at modern Bergama. On the way we passed through thousands of acres of figs that are marketed world-wide as 'Smyrna' figs. Our immediate interest was in the old city of Pergamos. At one time Pergamos could boast the largest library in the world. Antony gave it to Cleopatra but unfortunately it was destroyed in the fire of Alexandria which consumed the treasures from Pergamos as well as like treasures from the famous library of Alexandria.

The name Pergamos means elevation. The city and fortress were built on the top of a hill. However, the locals had a gymnasium down on the plains where there is still an abundance of spring water today which is claimed to be enhanced with healing properties.

John's letter rings out with disappointment at the compromise found at Pergamos. Revelation 2:14-17. '"Nevertheless, I have a few things against you: You have people there who hold to the teaching of Balaam, who taught Balak to entice the Israelites to sin by eating food sacrificed to idols and by committing sexual immorality. Likewise you also have those who hold to the teaching of the Nicolaitans."' If the members of the church were faithful then, '"I will give some of the hidden manna. I will also give him a white stone with a new name written on it, known only to him who receives it."'

All around Pergamos is white stone — marble or quartz. It was prized by the locals and others too. It is suggested that the Pergamos period is between the fourth and sixth centuries which was a time of great compromise in Christianity. The old foundations were shaken severely during this time.

THYATIRA

The Roman road goes inland from Pergamos and soon we came to the few ruins that are left of Thyatira. In the New

3

1 An arch, still intact, on the edge of the market place at Smyrna.
2 A Hittite lion in the market place.
3 On top of the Acropolis at Pergamos (Pergamum) are reconstructions of temples and administrative buildings.

1

2

King James Version of the Bible there is a heading at the beginning of this letter to Thyatira. It simply read, 'The corrupt church'. This was the middle church, the persecuted church. Even in Turkey there are remains, particularly in Cappadocia, of Christian hideouts. The underground cities of Kaymakli, Dolav Hani and Derinkuya as well as the six churches in the open air museum of Goreme speak volumes of this period of Church history.

There is some commendation for this church. Revelation 2:19, '"I know your deeds, your love and faith, your service and perseverance, and that you are now doing more than you did at first."' Even though there was gross corruption, there was still a message of comfort to those who were not corrupted by the worldly influences that had crept into the church. Notice it: Revelation 2:25-28: '"Only

hold on to what you have until I come. To him who overcomes and does my will to the end, I will give authority over the nations — 'He will rule them with an iron sceptre; he will dash them to pieces like pottery' — just as I have received authority from my Father. I will also give him the morning star."' Even today there are quite significant pottery works not far from Thyatira.

In the Christian Church time clock, this church period was from the sixth to the sixteenth centuries. This was a time of corruption and illiteracy in the world and

3

in the Church. Many have thought that during this church period the 'morning star' represents the period of the Reformation begun in England by John Wyclif.

SARDIS

A few miles down the Roman road it is not difficult to see Sart, a modern name for Sardis. In the days of Cyrus of Persia, Sardis was known as having a well-nigh impregnable fortress. This daunting obstacle presented a challenge to overcome, and one of Cyrus' soldiers climbed the wall at night and opened the gates of the city to the Persian armies. Today there is a lot of archaeological work taking place and with it a lot of rebuilding. Mosaic floors have been found from Roman times. Foundations and columns of a huge temple still remain. John's letter indicates that the church itself appeared to be dead. Even so there remain some who were faithful: Revelation 3:4, 5: '"Yet you have a few people in Sardis who have not soiled their clothes. They will walk with me, dressed in white for they are worthy. He who overcomes will, like them, be dressed in white. I will never erase his name from

69

the book of life, but will acknowledge his name before my Father and his angels."' A wonderful promise for the Church era which was about to see a revival.

PHILADELPHIA

John's next letter was written to Philadelphia. This name means 'brotherly love'. There is really little left of old Philadelphia. I asked at a cafe for directions to the remaining ruins. A helpful gentleman came with me and showed me the very meagre ruins — some walls of the old city and foundations of a Byzantine church. He then took me to a place where beautiful aerated and sparkling spring water was coming straight out of the ground. We filled our water containers and were most grateful.

Later we mused that brotherly love was still very evident in this city which received no rebuke from the prophet's pen. Instead he gave much commendation. Notice a part of this: Revelation 3:8: "'I know your deeds. See, I have placed before you an open door that no one can shut. I know that you have little strength, yet you have kept my word and have not denied my name."' Then he adds a beautiful promise to those faithful to Christ and His Word. Verses 10, 11: "'Since you have kept my command to endure patiently, I will also keep you from the hour of trial that is going to come upon the whole world to test those who live on the earth. I am coming soon. Hold on to what you have, so that no one will take your crown."'

1 Very little remains of old Philadelphia, however, the mode of transport has largely remained unchanged in the area.
2 Hierapolis was built on a mountainside of calcified rock. It has hot mineral springs from which water flows down to Laodicea, arriving lukewarm.

LAODICEA

We can still remember our first visit to Laodicea. We could look across the fields from the two amphitheatres, one very large, and see the white terraces of modern Pammukale. The springs there are really magnificent and very popular among tourists and those needing the benefits of the mineral waters. It was to the Laodiceans that John wrote the seventh letter.

Laodicea in those days was a large provincial city, boasting banks and a number of industries. As a city it was quite proud of its achievements. This pride was not lost in the church which is called lukewarm. Revelation 3:15-17: "'I know your deeds, that you are neither cold nor hot. I wish you were either one or the other! So, because you are lukewarm — neither hot nor cold — I am about to spit you out of my mouth. You say, 'I am rich; I have acquired wealth and do not need a thing.' But you do not realize that you are wretched, pitiful, poor, blind and naked.''' As you read this, it is not hard to realize that this was a stern rebuke to the church of the day. However, it also reminds us of the condition of the Christian Church today. But all is not lost! Verses 20, 21: '"Here I am! I stand at the door and knock. If anyone hears my voice and opens the door, I will go in and eat with him, and he with me. To him who overcomes, I will give the right to sit with me on my throne, just as I overcame and sat down with my Father on his throne."'

Holman Hunt got the inspiration from this text for his painting which is now hanging in Keeble College, Oxford. It pictures Christ knocking at a closed door. He is holding a lantern. The door has no handle, for it is the door to the human heart. Holman was commissioned to paint a second painting, the same as the first. This can be seen in St Paul's Cathedral, London.

CAPPADOCIA

If there are just seven wonders of the world then Cappadocia should be included. Its 96 kilometres (60 miles) of winding valleys with stalagmite pinnacles are a natural wonder. The valley was covered at one time with volcanic ash

People were in Jerusalem from Cappadocia when Peter was preaching at Pentecost (Acts 2:9). The Apostle Peter greets the church in Cappadocia in his epistle (1 Peter 1:1). When Christians fled here from the more coastal regions of Asia Minor, they tunnelled their way into the soft pumice and sandstone and created homes and churches. Archaeologists have found thousands of homes and in the Goreme Valley alone six churches. Today this area is known as the open air theatre. Most outstanding and hardest to photograph are the underground cities where thousands of people could remain protected. These were first started by the Hittites up to 2,000 years before Christ. They built the first two levels below the surface and then Christians added another six levels. These were all well supplied with fresh

from Mount Ericlyas. Rain, hail and snow have taken away the softer earth and left pumice and sandstone. In the sixth century AD Christians sought refuge here from the persecuting Romans and later the advancing Muslims. They lived here for at least another six centuries. The elevation is over 1,219 metres (4,000 feet) and for much of the year it is covered in snow.

air ducts as well as having an abundant water supply. The spiritual lives of the people were evidently well catered for with large meeting places and in the centre of one of the underground cities at Derinkuya is a large baptistery complete with water channels. A number of people could be baptized by immersion at one time. Two floors below this place where people buried their old life of sin symbolized by baptism, was a cemetery for their dead. The underground cities are undoubtedly the most exciting places in Cappadocia that we have visited.

celebrated meeting at this place. Paul the apostle was born here of Jewish parents who were already Roman citizens. This meant that he too was a Roman citizen and gave him ready 'visas' to visit so many countries on his celebrated missionary journeys.

BOGAZKOY (HITTITES)

Very little was known about the Hittites until the turn of the twentieth century. The name appears in nearly fifty scriptural references, but even so until concrete evidence surfaced, many critics

3

4

1 Here is the nunnery or lookout area guarding the six churches at Goreme.

2 Located in the province of Cappadocia were some forty underground cities. There is a baptistery at the ancient underground church of Derinkuya, where a number of people could be baptized by immersion at the same time.

3 Cleopatra's Gate, named after the celebrated meeting of Cleopatra and Antony at Tarsus.

4 These earthenware vessels found at Bogazkoy, site of the ancient Hittite city of Hattusas, held oil and flour.

TARSUS

This was 'no mean city' as Paul says in Acts 21:39: 'Paul answered, "I am a Jew, from Tarsus in Cilicia, a citizen of no ordinary city."' It was a large provincial town. It is first mentioned in Hittite records around 2000 BC. Cyrus the younger camped here with 10,000 of his soldiers on his way to take the Persian crown. Antony and Cleopatra had their

wrote that the Hittites were simply a mythological race. Over thirty Hittite cities have now been excavated in Turkey, the country which was home for these people of Anatolia. When Tutankhamun died, his wife Ankhesenamun wrote to the king of the Hittites requesting his son to take Tutankhamun's place. The request was unusual. But the queen was only allowed ninety days to make her own

1 Hittite soldiers carved into a rock face at Bogazkoy (see picture 3).

2 The deer god of the Hittites set in the centre of a sun disc, possibly a symbol of royalty.

3 Hittite soldiers in the sanctuary area.

must have been very difficult for a young queen of only 19 years of age and probably a disappointment for the Hittites!

At Bogazkoy the Hittites established a large fortress. A large wall surrounded the city and inside there were several temples and a sanctuary. In the sanctuary which was built in the cleft of a cliff, we could clearly see in relief form some of the gods of the Hittites. Protecting the gods and the sanctuary is a remarkable relief, also in the cliff face, of Hittite soldiers — the only symbol yet found of Hittite soldiers. On the hill above the sanctuary was a walled citadel. Some of the gates are well preserved, such as the kings' gate and lions' gate, and a long secret tunnel that leads to the outside.

When critics were convincing the world that the Hittites were only a fabled race, archaeologists began digging up cities that yielded a treasure store of writings, reliefs, statues and artifacts. Another plus for the biblical writers!

choice. The time quickly passed by. When the truthfulness of the story had been checked and the necessary consent given, the queen had already been forced to take the choice of the Egyptian priests, a big fat old priest named Ay, and the ninety days of choice had passed. This

Greece

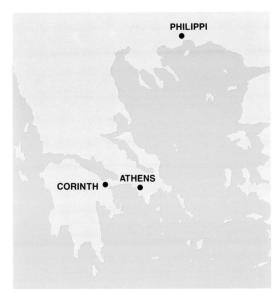

treatment they were praying and singing hymns to God and the other prisoners were listening to them! Acts 16:26-33: 'Suddenly there was such a violent earthquake that the foundations of the prison were shaken. At once all the prison doors flew open, and everybody's chains came loose. The jailer woke up, and when he saw the prison doors open, he drew his sword and was about to kill himself because he thought the prisoners had escaped. But Paul shouted, "Don't harm yourself! We are all here!" The jailer called for lights, rushed in and fell trembling before Paul and Silas. He then brought them out and asked, "Men, what must I do to be saved?" They replied, "Believe in the Lord Jesus, and you will be saved — you and your household."

PHILIPPI

ACTS 16:12-13: 'From there we travelled to Philippi, a Roman colony and the leading city of that district of Macedonia. And we stayed there several days. On the Sabbath we went outside the city gate to the river, where we expected to find a place of prayer. We sat down and began to speak to the women who had gathered there.' Later in Philippi they were put into gaol. Acts 16:23, 24: 'After they had been severely flogged, they were thrown into prison, and the jailer was commanded to guard them carefully. Upon receiving such orders, he put them in the inner cell and fastened their feet in the stocks.' Can you believe it, after that

The Magistrates Court in Philippi where Paul and Silas were tried.

Then they spoke the word of the Lord to him and to all the others in his house. At that hour of the night the jailer took them and washed their wounds; then immediately he and all his family were baptized.'

Archaeologists have done a lot of good work at Philippi, and in fact still have seasons of work there before everything is documented. It was a very large and important city and the river that was flowing in the days of Lydia and the gaoler and his family, is still there. The Orthodox Church has built a lovely little amphitheatre by the riverside at approximately the place where Paul would have held his baptisms.

2

ATHENS

While this was the most illustrious city of ancient Greece, there is no book of the Bible that addresses a church in Athens as for Philippi, Thessalonica and Corinth. The city is named after its patron goddess and records show that it was established around the sixteenth century BC. We have no account of any strong church being established in Athens in Paul's day. He visited the city on his second missionary journey and found that the Athenians were inquisitive about the gods (Acts 17:21-23).

Archaeologists and others have found something in the order of 3,000 statues in Athens and most of these appear to have been objects of worship. There has not been found an altar to 'the unknown god' such as Paul mentions in Acts 17:23, however in Pergamos an altar with this inscription has been discovered. It is clear that many of the ancients could not blame certain calamities on their treasured gods and so established altars to 'the unknown god'.

There was a Jewish synagogue in Athens and Paul preached there, as was his custom in commencing Christian work in a new city. There was little success at Athens even though he left a small group of Christians there, for among them was a high official and a woman of repute (Acts 17:32-34). While it is not mentioned in the scriptures, Paul would have surely come back again on his third missionary journey.

1 The riverside setting at Philippi where baptisms would have taken place.

2 The Agora or market place at Philippi.

3 The Parthenon dominates Athens. It has occupied the rock platform of the Acropolis since more than four centuries before Paul's visit.

4 The Odeion of Herodes Atticus, still in use, was one of the sites Paul would have viewed in Athens.

1

CORINTH CITY

Archaeologists have recovered an enormous amount of material and information from the ancient city of Corinth. Throughout the centuries this has been a splendid city neatly snuggling into a mountain that rises steeply to 548 metres (1,800 feet). On the top of the mountain was the acro-Corinth which contained a temple dedicated to Aphrodite and a citadel.

The fact that Corinth was a large city that had harbours on two gulfs, Cenchreae and Lechaeum, and a unique position at the top of the Peloponnesian peninsular, gave it prominence and wealth. American expeditions have worked here since 1896 and we now have an almost complete picture of the city. Statues (many headless), pottery vessels, coins and inscriptions have been found in

2

CORINTH CANAL

One of the amazing feats of engineering of the last century has been the building of the Corinth Canal. It was commenced in 1881 and finished in 1893. The emperor Nero in AD 67 first dreamed of this canal which would save a more than three hundred and twenty kilometre (two hundred mile) journey around the coast for his boats going to Asia Minor or across to Israel. Many ships were hauled across the isthmus to save the journey around the south of Greece. When it was finally completed last century it was 6.5 kilometres (4 miles) long, 21 metres (70 feet) wide and about 7.6 metres (25 feet) deep. This has allowed coastal freighters and small boats to save time, fuel and perhaps even shipwreck. It is worth stopping near the bridge and checking out; it is both unique and picturesque!

abundance. Today they adorn a museum in Corinth as well as museums in other parts of the world. An inscription has been found containing the name of Erastus; probably the same man named in Romans 16:23.

Paul came to Corinth on his second missionary journey and spent eighteen months helping to establish the church. He then spent another three months on his third journey. It was to this early Christian church in Corinth that Paul wrote two epistles, in fact his longest. In these epistles he covered much of the teachings understood by the church. It is evident that the church at Corinth was involved in some growing pains and needed these two epistles to set the members on a stable course for the growth of Christianity in the Corinth community. 1 Corinthians 1:10–4:21 covers factions that had arisen in the church and how they should be met. He goes on to cover moral irregularities, marriage relationships, food offered to idols, the Lord's supper, and spiritual gifts. His greatest chapter must be that of 1 Corinthians 13 which covers the supreme gift of love. 'Love never fails' and it must be at the centre of every action and motive in the Christian life. The Corinthians had seemingly bypassed this wonderful and most important gift. Perhaps much of Christianity today is still a 'resounding gong and clanging cymbals' and too has bypassed the best and foremost of the Spirit's fruits and gifts.

1 The Corinth Canal, a feat of nineteenth-century engineering that fulfilled Nero's dream.

2 The Lechaeum road through Corinth leads towards the mountain topped by the acro-Corinth containing a temple dedicated to Aphrodite, goddess of love.

3 The Jewish quarter, Corinth. After the decree of Emperor Claudius to expel Jews from Rome (Acts 18:2), large numbers settled in Corinth more so than in any other city.

INDEX *Page numbers in italic refer to captions.*